create
3 new
habits

A simple guide to form new habits
for a better, simpler, happier life

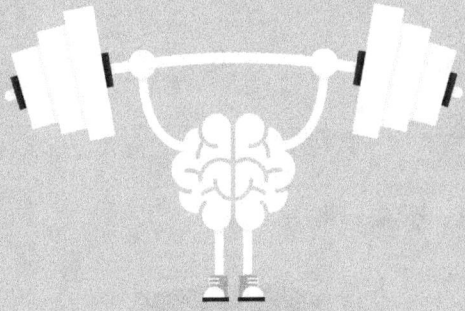

ja pérez

Create 3 New Habits
A simple guide to form new habits for a better, simpler, happier life.

© 2018 JA Pérez

All rights reserved. This book contains material protected under International and Federal Copyright Laws and Treaties. Any unauthorized reprint or use of this material is prohibited. No part of this book may be reproduced or transmitted in any form or by any means, electronic or mechanical, including photocopying, recording, or by any information storage and retrieval system without express written permission from the publisher.

For permission requests, write to the publisher, addressed "Attention: Permissions Coordinator," at the address below.

P.O. Box211325
Chula Vista, CA 91921 USA

Published by: Keen Sight Books
www.KeenSightBooks.com

Report errors to errata@keensightbooks.com

ISBN: 978-1947193161

Printed in the U.S.A.

Thanks to my daughter Amy Grace for her help with the corrections on this work.

Contents

Quick Intro. Why only 3 habits? 7

Chapter 1. Why Habits? 10
Chapter 2. How do we do this? 13
Chapter 3. Ready? Let's take the first step 16

My Daily Journal 17

Chapter 4. A list of good habits 62
Chapter 5. Why 3 things? 80
Chapter 6. Why 21 days? 83

After 21 days.. 87

Notes 91
About the author 97
Other Books by JA Pérez 99

Quick Intro

Why only 3 habits?

I'm sure there are many good habits that have been suggested to you before—habits that will improve your life in many areas.

You have probably read about habits that can improve productivity in the area of business, or eating and exercising habits to improve your health... habits that can help you have better relationships, or to simplify your life and create free time, minimize stress, have more energy, organize your day, and the list can go on and on.

It's overwhelming, isn't it?

Too many. Too much. That's exactly the problem. That's one of the reasons it is so hard making lasting changes to improve the way we live.

Most coaches that help you to make positive changes in your life, will start by asking you to create a list of all the changes you want to make. When you see in front of you that big mountain to conquer, you can't help but feel powerless, not knowing where to start.

So, why don't we just relax, and think about focusing on a less number of things. At least for now.

I find that when I simplify things I accomplish more.

The journey of a thousand miles begins with one step. —Lao Tzu

---

In this journey we'll focus on creating only three new habits. Why three?

Why not one, or four?

You could choose to just create one new habit at a time. I won't judge you. That may very well be a good number. You'll see below that we are not in a race to accomplish quantity here. You could also create a greater number of habits, if you like, and practice them at the same time. However, creating a greater number of habits at the same time can be overwhelming. The idea of this guide is to "keep it simple". I chose three, because I believe we can create three new habits at a time without losing simplicity, or adding stress.

You can read more about my research: Why 3 things on chapter 5.

Chapter 1

Why Habits?

Let me share with you some thoughts about why creating habits is so important for us to live a better, simpler, happier life.

However, if you don't worry much about the "why" for now and you feel you are ready to jump into action, go to day 1 of our journey and perhaps later come back to read the rest of this chapter.

Habits instead of goals

If you need to lose 20 pounds, that can be overwhelming. Why don't we just focus on losing some for now. We can create some healthy habits that in time will produce some results. Think about losing 1 pound, then celebrate that we have mastered that level and continue to practice your new habit. It could be a habit consisting in eating some kinds of foods instead of others, or a habit of taking long walks. As you continue to practice that habit, it will become easier and easier, and eventually you will reap the good results, without stress, frustrations, or disappointments.

The idea of new habits is not to create high expectations, but a rhythm. High expectations will bring discouragement if the process seems to go slower than expected. That's why I say "forget about goals". Create a rhythm. A process that will take you there.

You'll see that as you walk on that path, you'll start to love the journey.

Don't rush it. Stop to smell the flowers, and before you know it, you'll arrive at that beautiful destination. And you'll arrive happy, full of joy and ready to create your next adventure.

Habits instead of resolutions

There is a park close to where I live. It's funny that every new year, the first few days of the year, as I go out to take a morning walk on a trail that starts behind that park, I see many people running around the park—one year I counted over 60 people.

It's interesting that by the second week of the year,

that number starts to go down, and by the third week, you find that the number of runners has gone down to the usual 4 of 5 people that usually run there the rest of the year.

What happened to the large number of enthusiastic runners that were there the first few days of the year?

Well. Those were the ones that started the year with a set of new year resolutions.

It's interesting to see how fast people will break those new year resolutions, only to fall in guilt, and discouragement.

I'd like to show you a better way.

Forget New Year Resolutions. Forget about setting goals. How about we setup a system. A journey. A way of life where the process is the goal.

Instead of worrying about reaching a goal, why don't we just focus in the joy of slowly looking to the life around us as we walk on that path.

That's what creating new habits is all about. It's about creating a rhythm that allows us to enjoy the life around us as we focus on the things that are important to us and learn to let go of all the distractions that rob us of real joy, peace and contentment.

Chapter 2

How do we do this?

To create a new habit, we need to repeat it several times until it becomes part of our daily routine.

There are studies that show that it takes at least 21 days repeating something for it to become a habit, so, this is the system we'll use on a daily basis. If you like to read more about why 21 days, go to chapter six. So 21 days can be a good idea, but you don't have to stop there, you might want to keep practicing the routine past the 21 days. For now we'll base your first cycle on 21 days. You can use this same guide to create another three new habits after you have established the first three, but don't worry about that. For now, we'll just focus on three habits.

Every day you will do three things using the daily guide. The three things you will do are, read, write, and practice.

As soon as you wake up in the morning do this:

1- Read the habit phrase for the day and the encouragement paragraph of the day.

2- Write down the three habits we are creating. The same three. That means that you'll write the same three things every day, using the work pages included in this guide.

For example: My 3 new habits are: 1- Read a book 30 minutes every day (to increase my education). 2- Give someone else one complement daily (improving relationships). 3- Take a daily long walk (to maintain my health).

So then, every day, for the next 21 days, I will write down those three habits in my daily journal (this book). In other words when you go back and look at previous days, all pages will have the same three habits written on them, so that the habits portion on all pages will look the same each day.

After you write down your three habits on today's page, close this book and go practice the habits. In my case, I would go read for 30 minutes, then go for a long walk, and give someone a compliment. Though, not necessarily in that order (see more example habits on page 62).

3- Go practice your three new habits. Don't rush it. Take your time.

After you practice your three habits for the day, then come back to the day number and write a little more. Write down your thoughts for the day.

Is there a joy or peace you feel as a result of practicing your habits this day? Or anything else you want to say? Write it down. Remember this is a journey.

*You may chose to write down your thoughts as soon as you complete practicing the habits, or at night before you go to sleep.

Chapter 3

Ready?
Let's take the first step

Choosing my new habits

It is very possible that you already have some good habits you want to implement in your life. If that's the case, then just go to day 1 and write down your three new habits.

If you are not sure yet, or you need help deciding what new habits can be good for you at this time in your life, then go to page 62. Read the comprehensive list of good habits and how they can help you and in what area of your life.

MY DAILY JOURNAL

Day 1

Phrase for the day

"We are what we repeatedly do. Excellence, then, is not an act, but a habit." – Aristotle

Encouragement

Today, you and I start a journey. It will not be a perfect one, but it's fine. If you fail to repeat your new habits one day, don't judge yourself too hard. Don't allow guilt to come in. Failing is part of the process. So, give yourself permission to fail and in that space you will succeed.

Now, go on, write your three new habits. Everything is in your favor.

My 3 new habits are:

1_____

2_____

3_____

Now close the book and go practice your 3 new habits. Come back later to write down your thoughts.

My thoughts:

_____

_____

_____

_____

_____

_____

_____.

Day 2

Phrase for the day

> "A nail is driven out by another nail; habit is overcome by habit." — Desiderius Erasmus

Encouragement

Relax, take your time.

Too much busyness keeps us from becoming who we might have become, had we given ourselves the space. This is a tricky reality for modern enterprises and the people tasked with strategic thinking within them[1].

Today we slow down. Look around, life is wonderful.

My 3 new habits are:

(the same 3 new habits you wrote yesterday)

    1 _____

    2 _____

    3 _____

Now close the book and go practice your 3 new habits. Come back later to write down your thoughts.

My thoughts:

_____

_____

_____

_____

_____

_____

_____ .

Day 3

Phrase for the day

"Your beliefs become your thoughts, Your thoughts become your words, Your words become your actions, Your actions become your habits, Your habits become your values, Your values become your destiny." —Mahatma Gandhi

---

Encouragement

Choose Simplicity.

Chaos will always be easier than simplicity to achieve. As a result, we will often feel frazzled, with our backs against the wall. You need to give yourself time to concentrate[2].

My 3 new habits are:

(the same 3 new habits you wrote yesterday)

1_____

2_____

3_____

Now close the book and go practice your 3 new habits. Come back later to write down your thoughts.

My thoughts:

_____
_____
_____
_____
_____
_____.

Day 4

Phrase for the day

"We become what we repeatedly do."
—Sean Covey

Encouragement

Most of our lives are spent following unconscious, habitual patterns. We wake and start immediately with our usual distractions. Fall into regular eating habits, interact with people reactively out of old mental patterns, and constantly thinking of something other than what we're doing out of habit.

Today we make a conscious decision to step away from those old habitual patterns, by paying attention and replacing them by our new three healthy habits.

Enjoy your day. You are doing great!

My 3 new habits are:

(the same 3 new habits you wrote yesterday)

1_____

2_____

3_____

Now close the book and go practice your 3 new habits. Come back later to write down your thoughts.

My thoughts:

_____

_____

_____

_____

_____

_____

_____.

Day 5

Phrase for the day

> *"Enthusiasm is the electricity of life. How do you get it? You act enthusiastic until you make it a habit."* —Gordon Parks

Encouragement

Enthusiasm does not happen automatically. It takes practice and repetition. The more you put into action, having an enthusiastic attitude, the easier it becomes to make it a constant characteristic of your personality.

Try practicing enthusism today, and tomorrow, and the day after. Practice your 3 new habits enthusiastically. It will be fun!

My 3 new habits are:

(the same 3 new habits you wrote yesterday)

1_____

2_____

3_____

Now close the book and go practice your 3 new habits. Come back later to write down your thoughts.

My thoughts:

_____
_____
_____
_____
_____
_____
_____.

Day 6

Phrase for the day

"Good habits are worth being fanatical about." —John Irving

Encouragement

Smile at your 3 new habits. They are like 3 new friends, waiting daily to enjoy your company. They are becoming part of your life, part of you. Enjoy this day!

My 3 new habits are:

(the same 3 new habits you wrote yesterday)

1_____

2_____

3_____

Now close the book and go practice your 3 new habits. Come back later to write down your thoughts.

My thoughts:

_____
_____
_____
_____
_____
_____
_____.

Day 7

Phrase for the day

> "The best kind of happiness is a habit you're passionate about."
> —Shannon L. Alder

Encouragement

Hang out with people who believe in your new habits. You don't have to tell people about your new habits if you chose not to. But, if you have friends that want what is good for you, it is always a good idea to share with someone what you are doing. It is also a way of keeping you accountable. Just make sure it is someone who supports you and believes in what you are doing. Stay away from negative people. Pray for them, love them, but from a distance.

My 3 new habits are:

(the same 3 new habits you wrote yesterday)

1_____

2_____

3_____

Now close the book and go practice your 3 new habits. Come back later to write down your thoughts.

My thoughts:

_____
_____
_____
_____
_____
_____
_____.

Day 8

Phrase for the day

> "Just do it! First you make your habits, then your habits make you!" —Lucas Remmerswaal

Encouragement

Stop negative self-talk. I'm not asking you to keep your head in the sand and ignore life's less pleasant situations. Just to practice approaching unpleasantness in a more productive way, by not allowing an endless stream of unspoken negative thoughts to run through your head. Practice positive self-talk. Start by following one simple rule: Don't say anything to yourself that you wouldn't say to anyone else. Be gentle and encouraging with yourself. If a negative thought enters your mind, evaluate it rationally and respond with affirmations of what is good about you. Think about things you're thankful for in your life.

My 3 new habits are:

(the same 3 new habits you wrote yesterday)

1_____

2_____

3_____

Now close the book and go practice your 3 new habits. Come back later to write down your thoughts.

My thoughts:

_____
_____
_____
_____
_____
_____
_____.

Day 9

Phrase for the day

> "Good habits are the key to all success. Bad habits are the unlocked door to failure." —Og Mandino

Encouragement

Today will be a good day. Not perfect, but just good. This morning we are setting the tone for the rest of the day. Almost invariably, we're going to encounter obstacles throughout the day—there's no such thing as a perfect day. When we encounter such a challenge, we will focus on the benefits, no matter how slight or unimportant they seem. For example, if I get stuck in traffic, that will give me the time to listen a good podcast. If the store is out of the food I want to eat, I'll think about the thrill of trying something new. With God's help, "today will be a good day".

My 3 new habits are:

(the same 3 new habits you wrote yesterday)

1_____

2_____

3_____

Now close the book and go practice your 3 new habits. Come back later to write down your thoughts.

My thoughts:

_____
_____
_____
_____
_____
_____
_____.

Day 10

Phrase for the day

> "Habits are safer than rules; you don't have to watch them. And you don't have to keep them either. They keep you." —Frank Crane

Encouragement

Did you forget to pick up the milk on your way home? Did you forget an important phone call you had to make? Don't feel bad about the things you forgot to do. It happens to all humans. Instead, try making time to write down things. Writing things down can foster a sense of achievement and progress, expanding our possibilities and increasing our productivity. Writing things down will free memory space so you can concentrate on important things and think big.

My 3 new habits are:

(the same 3 new habits you wrote yesterday)

1_____

2_____

3_____

Now close the book and go practice your 3 new habits. Come back later to write down your thoughts.

My thoughts:

_____
_____
_____
_____
_____
_____
_____.

Day 11

Phrase for the day

> *"All our life, so far as it has definite form, is but a mass of habits."* —William James

Encouragement

Today, you will have accomplished more than half of the 21 days on creating these 3 new habits. It probably hasn't been perfect. You might have failed some along the way, but I'm here to tell you it is all fine. Don't lose enthusiasm. Winston Churchill once said: "Success consists of going from failure to failure without losing enthusiasm." Today I want to remind you that, even if you may be feeling a bit like a failure, you are most definitely not. You are still here and you are reading this. You are doing really good.

My 3 new habits are:

(the same 3 new habits you wrote yesterday)

1_____

2_____

3_____

Now close the book and go practice your 3 new habits. Come back later to write down your thoughts.

My thoughts:

_____
_____
_____
_____
_____
_____
_____.

Day 12

Phrase for the day

> "Character is simply habit long continued." —Plutarch

Encouragement

We are not born into this world with fixed habits. Neither do we inherit a noble character. Instead, we are given the privilege and opportunity of choosing which way of life we will follow—which habits we will form.

"Because bad habits provide some type of benefit in your life, it's very difficult to simply eliminate them. (This is why simplistic advice like "just stop doing it" rarely works.)

Instead, you need to replace a bad habit with a new habit that provides a similar benefit. —James Clear[3]

In this path by creating healthy new habits, you are growing and maturing in character.

My 3 new habits are:

(the same 3 new habits you wrote yesterday)

1_____

2_____

3_____

Now close the book and go practice your 3 new habits. Come back later to write down your thoughts.

My thoughts:

_____
_____
_____
_____
_____
_____
_____.

Day 13

Phrase for the day

"Freely chosen, discipline is absolute freedom." —Ron Serino

Encouragement

Happiness is not: Feeling good all the time, or being rich, or affording everything you want. A research[4] suggests that happiness is a combination of how satisfied you are with your life (for example, finding meaning in your work) and how good you feel on a day-to-day basis. You have the ability to control how you feel—and with consistent practice, you can form lifelong habits for a more satisfying and fulfilling life. Have a great day!

My 3 new habits are:

(the same 3 new habits you wrote yesterday)

1_____

2_____

3_____

Now close the book and go practice your 3 new habits. Come back later to write down your thoughts.

My thoughts:

_____
_____
_____
_____
_____
_____
_____.

Day 14

Phrase for the day

> *"Winning is a habit. Unfortunately, so is losing."* —Vince Lombardi

Encouragement

Life is a process. Life is not about the outcome or the destination. It is truly about the journey. It is about your personal growth, understanding of it, and how you apply what you learn to your life.

My 3 new habits are:

(the same 3 new habits you wrote yesterday)

1_____

2_____

3_____

Now close the book and go practice your 3 new habits. Come back later to write down your thoughts.

My thoughts:

_____
_____
_____
_____
_____
_____
_____.

Day 15

Phrase for the day

> "Your net worth to the world is usually determined by what remains after your bad habits are subtracted from your good ones." —Benjamin Franklin

Encouragement

There are no shortcuts in personal development. There are no shortcuts when it comes to creating healthy habits. What I can offer you is this: If you do something every day, that action will slowly become a habit. That's it. That simple. One day at a time. One step at a time.

My 3 new habits are:

(the same 3 new habits you wrote yesterday)

1. _____

2. _____

3. _____

Now close the book and go practice your 3 new habits. Come back later to write down your thoughts.

My thoughts:

_____
_____
_____
_____
_____
_____
_____.

Day 16

Phrase for the day

"A large part of virtue consists in good habits." —Barbara Paley

Encouragement

Success in life tends to be associated with one-time big things, but that way of thinking is wrong. Instead, success in all areas of life has far more to do with the little things you do habitually. Like for example, eating healthy meals daily, completing your biggest task at the beginning of the day before you check your email, etc... It is okay to form new habits slowly. Do not hurry. Time is on your side.

My 3 new habits are:

(the same 3 new habits you wrote yesterday)

1_____

2_____

3_____

Now close the book and go practice your 3 new habits. Come back later to write down your thoughts.

My thoughts:

_____
_____
_____
_____
_____
_____
_____.

Day 17

Phrase for the day

> Motivation is what gets you started. Habit is what keeps you going. —Jim Ryun

Encouragement

Motivation alone is not going to get us too far. Consistent action is the only way we are going to get ahead, and for action to be consistent, it has to be habitual. Creating a workflow, a system of routines will help you find joy in the process and will keep you going.

My 3 new habits are:

(the same 3 new habits you wrote yesterday)

1_____

2_____

3_____

Now close the book and go practice your 3 new habits. Come back later to write down your thoughts.

My thoughts:

_____
_____
_____
_____
_____
_____
_____.

Day 18

Phrase for the day

Feeling sorry for yourself, and your present condition, is not only a waste of energy but the worst habit you could possibly have. —Dale Carnegie

Encouragement

Feeling sorry for yourself, or poor inside, does not help you accomplish anything. It arises because you feel no one is giving you the attention you want or helping you get out of your difficulties. The good news is that you can get out of the self-pity cycle by gathering some riches. I don't mean money, I mean collecting a list of your strengths. Write down each good quality you have and consider how to gained it. Write down what you are grateful for[5]. The next time you feel sorry for yourself, or in any way feel inadequate, take out your list.

My 3 new habits are:

(the same 3 new habits you wrote yesterday)

1_____

2_____

3_____

Now close the book and go practice your 3 new habits. Come back later to write down your thoughts.

My thoughts:

_____
_____
_____
_____
_____
_____
_____.

Day 19

Phrase for the day

> *Choose the life that is most useful, and habit will make it the most agreeable.*
> —Francis Bacon

Encouragement

Many people think that habits will help you achieve the type of life you want for yourself. That might be true in one level, but I have seen that good habits will help you discover purpose in the things you repeatedly do. Creating a rhythm that allows you to do them peacefully and joyfully.

My 3 new habits are:

(the same 3 new habits you wrote yesterday)

1_____

2_____

3_____

Now close the book and go practice your 3 new habits. Come back later to write down your thoughts.

My thoughts:

_____
_____
_____
_____
_____
_____
_____.

Day 20

Phrase for the day

> "Acquire the habit of speaking to God as if you were alone with Him, familiarly and with confidence and love, as to the dearest and most loving of friends." —Alphonsus Liguori

Encouragement

Many teachers will guide you to discover peace in your inner being. I say, that if the inside is empty, you'll be better off looking on the outside and away. If you feel God is away and far, start by talking to Him and then bringing the conversation closer until He and the conversation reside on the inside[6].

My 3 new habits are:

(the same 3 new habits you wrote yesterday)

1_____

2_____

3_____

Now close the book and go practice your 3 new habits. Come back later to write down your thoughts.

My thoughts:

_____
_____
_____
_____
_____
_____
_____.

Day 21

Phrase for the day

There is no influence like the influence of habit. —Gilbert Parker

Encouragement

Wow! We have arrived at day 21. I'm so proud of you. We have walked this journey together. By now most have created a good rhythm on repeating these 3 good habits every day. This is not the end of the road, nor graduation day. You must continue to practice these habits. You cannot sit down and expect the new habits to carry you automatically. Movement always starts with you. Now, please go on to practice today's habits, when you come back at the end of the day, I have a few more words for you.

My 3 new habits are:

(the same 3 new habits you wrote yesterday)

1_____

2_____

3_____

Now close the book and go practice your 3 new habits. Come back later to write down your thoughts.

My thoughts:

_____
_____
_____
_____
_____
_____
_____.

Okay, I have completed this 21 days guide. Now what?

My goal with this book has been to give you confidence and get you going. Now you know how to get going and as you keep practicing, these habits will become more and more a part of your life. To keep adding days, please feel free to make copies of the "after 21 days" page at the end of this book and keep using it for as long as you need or want. Or get a second book and start all over again if you want to repeat the same process. With the same habits or add 3 new habits to your life.

Final words

Thank you for taking the time to walk with me during these past 21 days. I wish you great success in everything you do. I believe you have great days ahead.

If this simple book has helped you in any way, please go to the book's page in Amazon.com and write a review. I read all reviews and I really appreciate your comments.

Blessings,

To keep reading

At the beginning of this book I didn't want to bore you with a lot of information or waste any time. I wanted to get you started on the 21 days guide right away. Now, if you would like to get some ideas about other good new habits, learn why I only choose 3 new habits at a time, or why this guide is 21 days, please read on, or if you might just want to keep practicing your new habits using the "after 21 days" page, it's totally fine, you may do so.

Chapter 4

A list of good habits

Spiritual Habits

Praying

A praying habit. Create the habit of praying daily. Praying is talking to God. You can start with praying 5 minutes a day.

Recommended free resources:

- Our Deepest Prayer: Hallowed Be Your Name by John Piper[7]
- Praying for a Breakthrough by John Piper[8]
- Experience the Presence: Prayer is experiencing the presence of God by The Navigators[9]

- How to Jump Start Your Prayer Battery by Kim Butts [10]

- Beginning a Life of Prayer by PrayerPower Radio [11]

- Ten Minutes with the Lord: Start Where You Are by Kaye Johns [12]

- Prayer of Salvation: Our First Real Conversation With God by All About God [13]

- Prayer 101: How Do I Talk to God? by BGEA [14]

- 10 Morning Prayers to Use Daily by Crosswalk Editorial Staff [15]

- Seven Simple Daily Prayers by Marshall Segal [16]

Reading the Bible

Reading the Bible to help you grow spiritually. Start reading a few verses a day, and as you start to enjoy it increase it to a chapter a day.

Recommended resources:

- How to Read the Bible by Wikihow [17]

- How to Read the Bible by NLT [18]

- The Bible in Basic English by Bible Study Tools [19]

- The Bible in One Year by Alpha International[20]

About *The Bible in One Year* guides and programs

If you are an avid reader, a guide for reading the Bible in one year might be good for you, however, can be overwhelming for some of us.

The idea of having to complete something out of obligation or a self imposed goal can become legalistic and create pressure or even anxiety.

I suggest that if you decide to make a habit of reading the Bible, you find the method that works for you.

For myself, I find it easier to read a book of the Bible and cross references when I find a theme or event interesting. For example, I might be reading about the prophet Elijah when he resurrected a young man, then I'll mark the passage and go look for other instances of resurrections that happened in other times and are recorded in other books of the Bible. Therefore my study becomes more thematic and less mechanical.

I encourage you to develop your own system.

Practice silence

Create the habit of being quiet and in tranquility. Turn off your phone, get away from the noise, go sit outside. Start by doing this 5 minutes a day, then increase it as you enjoy it more.

You don't have to become a monk to learn how to practice silence. And, I'm not talking silence as a meditation or necessarily a religious practice.

In a world full on noise, traffic, and electronics, it has become the norm to be listening to something all the time. When we get in the car, we turn on the radio. If we go for a walk, we put on our headphones and listen to music, or news, or even something inspirational that in itself can be really good and fun. I don't have anything against radios, or music, or even television.

On the other hand, I have experimented with this practice and learned to be in silence and can tell you that it is healthy and calming to turn off the noise once in awhile or as often as possible.

How do I do it?

Just get up from your desk and go outside to the office patio, or your backyard, and sit. Do nothing. Contemplate what's going on around you. The birds, the wind, or nothing. Just be there for 5 minutes.

When you go for a walk, try leaving your phone behind. Turn it off and put it away. The world is not going to end. Remember, there was life before there were cell phones. A quiet walk can be refreshing and inspiring.

Always start small, as with any other practice.

Productivity Habits

Pay one bill daily

When they are all paid, pay something in advance, or visit your bank account to make some financial planning, save money, etc... The idea is to not allow your bills to pile up, which can bring stress and make you feel overwhelmed. This is also a good practice to get out of debt.

I'm not talking about breaking a bill into small payments. I've read of financial advisers that say it makes no difference to your credit score if you pay a bill twice a month or weekly as long as you are never late. Barry Paperno writes in a post titled, Your low-limit secured card strategy: Pay the bill early, often:

"I like your method of frequent payments throughout the monthly billing cycle more than simply waiting for the monthly statement before paying[21]." So that can be a good idea although I would advise you to seek professional counsel when it comes to financial decisions. Now, the idea of practicing "paying a bill daily" or at least dedicating a few minutes every day to your personal finances, is that you don't leave or procrastinate checking up on your bills until the end of the month. Neglecting to check on your financial responsibilities often can result in you forgetting to make a payment on time and having you credit score affected, besides paying late fees which is never a good idea.

Schedule your priorities... Schedule everything

It can be a good habit to plan the day ahead. I like to schedule things and that's not necessarily all work. Yes I schedule things to do, tasks, meetings. I schedule travel time to a meeting to make sure I don't have to rush through traffic. I even try to schedule extra time when traveling. If there is an accident on the freeway and I get stuck in traffic, I don't have to be all stressed out because I know I have extra time. If flying, you know how common it is for a flight to be delayed due to weather conditions or any other number of reasons.

I schedule breaks in between tasks or meetings, time to go for coffee, time to just sit and be quiet.

When it comes to priorities, I don't look first at what's already in the schedule and then prioritize. I first think of what are my priorities in life and schedule them first.

The key is not to prioritize what's on your schedule, but to schedule your priorities.

I'm not perfect at it. I'm still learning and as prioritizing and scheduling is something I do repeatedly, than it needs to be a habit. A good habit.

Check your Emails once or twice a day

Make the habit of checking your Emails once or twice a day.

The bad habit of checking your inbox every few minutes takes a lot of time out of your workflow. It's a fact that every time you check your Emails, it will take you a few minutes to get back to what you were doing. When you add up all the time it takes you to get back and concentrate on your work multiplied by all the times you checked your inbox, you'll notice you lose one or two hours daily.

According to some experts, checking your email too frequently is actually a major factor that can contribute to diminished productivity[22].

According to one poll[23], about 40% of people surveyed that they thought they checked their email between 6 and 20 times per day.

So, how do we reduce distraction and assure productivity? There are different things people do to address this problem.

Let's look at two different methods:

1- Never Check Your Email in the Morning

Oprah's favorite organizational expert is a woman called Julie Morgenstern, author of "Never Check Email in the Morning[24]." Guess what she advises?

According to Morgenstern, checking your email first thing when you get into the office each morning is problematic because it can form a false sense of accomplishment. You answer 40 emails, and you feel like you've done a lot of work, but in reality you probably still have piles of paperwork, meetings, and phone calls to make.

2- The 24-Hour Method

Other people argue that you should just check them

once per day, in the morning. Among the members of this camp is productivity expert Elizabeth Grace Saunders[25]. She generally clears out her inbox during the first 1-2 hours of her day, and formulates her game plan for the rest of the day after that. After that, she doesn't generally look at her email again for the rest of the day, allowing her to focus completely on business development and client projects.

My method

If there is an important Email I'm waiting for, yes I'll check my inbox first thing in the morning. If I don't find the remittent or subject related by, I look at the unread Emails (in my system they appear in a bold font), I'll close my Email client right away. Then, I'll check again after lunch.

If I'm not waiting for something important, then I won't open my Email client in the morning. When I sit on my desk, I go right away to my 3 items to-do list and work on completing those 3 items on the first 5 hours of the day—as humans we only have about 5 really productive hours per day.

Then after lunch, or an early afternoon, I check my inbox and respond to the Emails. That's it. One time per day.

My associates and my team know my routine, so they don't expect an answer from me right away.

By the way, I don't answer to all Emails. It would be impossible. On any day I could receive from 15 to 200 Emails in my inbox. There is no way that I can answer all. I don't answer to advertising, to people I don't know, and I automate a lot of my correspondence. That way, I only answer from 5 to 7 Emails daily.

Automation

A great amount of correspondence we receive at our organization (not my personal inbox) is related to subscriptions, logistics related to our conferences and projects and people asking for help.

All subscriptions to our websites, newsletters, book offers, etc... are handled by an automated system that sends confirmations, thank you letters, directions to download, or directions to frequently asked questions. All correspondence directed to logistics are received by our team member in charge of logistics and communications.

Emails from individuals asking questions or asking for help are handled by the team member in charge of support.

With that structure in place, I'm free to pray, write, walk, prepare my conferences, invest time in our humanitarian projects, and have free time for family. Maybe to go out and have coffee with friends, or perhaps do a little bit of gardening–something I love doing.

It's not always easy. There can be some long complicated days at the office. Life is not perfect, but at least we plan and develop a process and that is important.

Get up early

As author Laura Vanderkam[26] studied the schedules of a number of high achievers. She found out the one thing they all had in common. They get up early, and almost all of them have a morning routine.

Richard Branson—an advocate of embracing the morning says: "I have always been an early riser. Like keeping a positive outlook, or keeping fit, waking up early is a habit, which you must work on to maintain. Over my 50 years in business I have learned that if I rise early I can achieve so much more in a day, and therefore in life[27]."

Make a 3 items TO-DO list

A long to-do list can be overwhelming. Instead, just make a short list.

The short list approach will keep you focused on the most important tasks you need to accomplish.

Yes, yes, I know, you have many things to complete, projects, tasks under each project and deadlines for those projects.

As you know, we cannot rely on memory—I used to go without writing down my "things to do' for many years, I could keep everything I needed to do in my memory, just the way I used to remember all of my friend's and relative's phone numbers by heart. But it is normal that as you age, you rely more on writing things down and it is for sure a good practice for young and old.

I see my to-do list as a second memory.

So, how do I create an effective to-do list that is practical, efficient and never overwhelming?

What I do is, I have a list of all long term projects, and there are many tasks to complete for each project. You can name this list whatever you like. I name mine "Ongoing".

So, yes, you are actually creating and working with two lists, but the idea is that you will only have the immediate attention on one list, that way, your energy and concentration is only put into that list, and because it's a short list, it will not be overwhelming.

The key to creating a non-overwhelming to-do list is knowing what's important, what's needed immediately and what can wait. There are things that are important but can wait, and there are things that are important and need to be completed as soon as possible.

Those things that are important and need to be completed sooner, you copy into your to-do list. I chose to only have 3 things in that list. If I'm able to complete the 3 things on the list early in the day and have time to do more, I can add one more from my Ongoing list, or just take off, go for a walk, enjoy the sun, celebrate that I completed 3 things.

For me, the 3-Item list provides a sense of accomplishment at the end of the day.

Why 3 items. Why not 2 or 4?

I use for this the same science I use for creating 3 new habits. See Why 3 things on page 80.

By the way, after doing this for awhile, I have found others doing similar things to minimize their workflow and enjoy life more.

Melissa Camara Wilkins[28] call it "An Enough List", and this is what she says about how it works for her:

"Now instead of ending each day feeling like I've fallen behind, I have a built-in sense of accomplishment in the evenings. I finished my three things! I did what mattered most!"

Joshua Becker[29] says this about a 3 items list:

"The importance of identifying the three most important things to accomplish in a day is revolutionary regardless of where you apply it. It is a helpful productivity hack at work."

Healthy Habits

Take long walks

Dr. Mercola says[30]: "If you want to add seven years to your lifespan, set aside 20 to 25 minutes for a daily walk. This simple habit, which can also arguably be one of the most enjoyable parts of your day, has been found to trigger an anti-aging process and even help repair old DNA."

What Are the Benefits of Regular Walking?

Author Sanjay Sharma, professor of inherited cardiac diseases in sports cardiology at St. George's University Hospitals NHS Foundation Trust in London, told The Independent[31]:

"We may never avoid becoming completely old, but we may delay the time we become old. We may look younger when we're 70 and may live into our nineties.

Exercise buys you three to seven additional years of life. It is an antidepressant, it improves cognitive function, and there is now evidence that it may retard the onset of dementia."

So, walking in general 20 to 25 minutes a day is a healthy habit.

Why long walks, in my case

Researchers found walking is just as good as running in reducing risk of high blood pressure, high cholesterol and diabetes.

A brisk long walk is as good as a run for cutting the risk of heart disease, researchers say.

This is because the most important factor is not intensity but the total energy used. So long as the energy used is similar, the health boost is similar, says a report in the American Heart Association journal Arteriosclerosis, Thrombosis and Vascular Biology.

Paul T Williams[32], of Lawrence Berkeley National Laboratory in California, said the findings were surprising but showed the key factor was the number of calories worked off in each form of activity. 'Walking and running provide an ideal test of the health benefits... because they involve the same muscle groups and the same activities performed at different intensities,' he said.

He estimates a person would need to walk 4.3 miles at a brisk pace to have the same amount of exercise as running 3 miles. It would take twice as long – around an hour and 15 minutes instead of 38 minutes' he said.

I like long walks, early in the morning or late at night, not only for the obvious health benefits I get when burning the calories. For me, long walks give me the opportunity to disconnect, specially if I leave my phone behind. No distractions, no noise. A time to reflect, to pray and to step aside from the business of the daily life and see things from a clear perspective.

These are some of the reasons I like long walks.

Now. You don't have to make this a habit, or you might chose to just take a 20 minute walk daily or 5 times a week.

Whatever works for you, but to make it a habit, it needs to be repeated consistently.

Eat Healthy

To eat healthy, we first have to understand which foods are actually healthy and which ones are not. We can learn from reading nutrition books and websites. Maybe even consult a dietitian to get you going.

It might take a more complicated process for some people, depending on your weight or other related medical challenges.

I'm not a nutritionist, and I will always tell you to consult your doctor before you make nutritional changes in your life.

My job here is not to tell you what to eat or what not to eat, but whenever you and your doctor decide on your diet program, you could use the guide presented in this book to make it a habit.

In the meantime, or before you see you doctor, there are some common sense ideas that can better your eating habits and that you could start to implement right away. For example, cutting down on fast food, on fried foods, on sugar, perhaps drinking more water.

The idea is to start somewhere.

You'll see that when you make it a habit on the small things, then it will be easier later when we move into make bigger changes in our life style.

Chapter 5

Why 3 things?

Why 3 things? Why not four or two?

Well. There is no science behind the number three. Or is it?

I haven't found any study yet on the psychology of doing three things and I don't want to make it a complicated science. The idea is to minimize, not to complicate things, right?

I see simple things in threes though.

Three strikes is one out in baseball. You have probably heard the phrase "as easy as one-two-three" which in the dictionary of idioms[33] means:

"To be extremely easy, simple, or intuitive; to require very little skill or effort."

More about 3 (if you have time to read it).

Three is a safe number, not too much, not too little, and for some reason, we humans do things in threes.

In the Olympics and other sporting events the winner of an event wins the gold medal. The athlete that comes in second gets the silver, and the one that is third receives the bronze. There is no medal for fourth, fifth, or beyond.

In business, we often look at things in three levels – optimistic, average, and pessimistic[34].

In probability theory, we look at high, medium and low probability cases.

When categorizing sales leads, we break them into three levels – Hot, Warm, and Cool; A, B, and C; or High, Medium, and Low.

In geometry, a triangle with three sides is the most stable shape. This is why bridges and buildings that must carry a lot of weight have structural elements based on triangles. In the scouts and the army, they teach you to triangulate your position so you don't get lost.

In writing The rule of three or power of three is a writing principle that suggests that things that come in threes are funnier, more satisfying, or more effective than other numbers of things[35].

Some examples:

- Life, Liberty and the Pursuit of Happiness, rights outlined in The Declaration of Independence

- Liberté, égalité, fraternité - The slogan of the French Republic predating 1790

- A Mars a day helps you to work, rest and play - Mars advertising slogan since 1959

- Stop, Look and Listen - A public road and level crossing safety slogan

- Stop, drop and roll, fire safety advice

Still not convinced of the power of three?

How about:

Three Stooges – Moe, Curly, and Larry. Three Musketeers – Athos, Porthos, and Aramis. Pep Boys – Manny, Moe, and Jack. Rice Krispies mascots – Snap, Crackle and Pop. Big 3 Broadcast Television Networks – ABC, CBS, and NBC.

Chapter 6

Why 21 days?

To create a new habit, we need to repeat it several times until it becomes part of our daily routine.

How long it takes a new habit to form can vary widely depending on several factors. Everybody is different, and everybody is under different circumstances.

There are studies that show that it takes at least 21 days repeating something for it to become a habit, but I don't believe those studies are completely accurate, nor I believe that one rule can apply to everybody. Again, everybody is different.

So, then, why did I make a 21-day guide for us to create 3 new habits?

First, I would like to establish that my guide is not a strict one. If you feel you need more than 21 days, please feel free to make a copy of the "after 21 days" page and keep using it for as long as you need or want, or get a second guide and start all over again.

The simple idea behind creating new habits is that as you repeat something, for a period of time, it becomes a habit.

Now, if you have time and would like to read more about some scientific studies about how long does it takes for a person to make a new habits and what different schools of thought say about it, here is some information.

21 days or more

In the 1950s Maxwell Maltz was a plastic surgeon when he began noticing a strange pattern among his patients.

When Dr. Maltz would perform a surgery he found that it would take the patient about 21 days to get used to the new changes. When a patient had a leg amputated, Maltz noticed that the patient would sense a phantom limb for about 21 days before adjusting to knowing the leg was no longer there..

He also noticed that it also took him about 21 days to form a new habit. Maltz wrote about these experiences and said, "These, and many other commonly observed phenomena tend to show that it requires a minimum of about 21 days for an old mental image to dissolve and a new one to jell[36]."

In the years that followed, Maltz's work influenced many "self-help" professionals from Zig Ziglar to Tony Robbins and as more people recited Maltz's story they began to forget that he said "a minimum of about 21 days" and shortened it to, "It takes 21 days to form a new habit[37]."

It's okay if it takes longer

A study was done in the European Journal of Social Psychology back in 2009 where each participant chose an eating, drinking, or other behavior to carry out daily, following a unique cue[38].

This activity was to be performed for 12 weeks.

The results? The average time it took for a behavior to become a habit was 66 days. But the surprising thing was the range of the data. For some participants it took just 18 days while others up to 254 days.

Like I said before. How long it takes to create a new habit is not a certain science. It is different for everybody depending on many factors.

The important thing is that it is certainly possible to create new habits, get rid of bad habits, and live a better, simpler, happier life.

Failing forward

On creating new habits, the journey can be messy. And it's okay.

If you fail one day, just take note, don't allow guilt to come inside your mind. Failing is not unique. It doesn't happen just to you. We all fail, and it's fine, as long as we learn something and move forward. I like best how C.S. Lewis said it:

> *"Failures, repeated failures, are finger posts on the road to achievement. One fails forward towards success."* —C.S. Lewis

After 21 days

Please feel free to make as many copies as you want of the following page and keep using it for as long as you need or want or get a second book guide and start all over again with another 3 new habits.

You can also download this "after 21 days" page from my site at:

https://japerez.com/english/habits/

Phrase for the day

(write down an inspirational phrase to start the day)

_____
_____
_____
_____
_____
_____.

Encouragement

(write some words of encouragement to help you start the day)

_____
_____
_____
_____
_____
_____.

My 3 new habits are:

(the same 3 new habits you wrote yesterday)

1. _____

2. _____

3. _____

Now close the book and go practice your 3 new habits. Come back later to write down your thoughts.

My thoughts

_____
_____
_____
_____
_____
_____
_____
_____.

Notes:

1- Entrepreneur Magazine. Give Yourself Space to Think Too much busyness keeps us from becoming who we might have become... https://www.entrepreneur.com/article/241745 (captured February 5, 2017)

2 - Entrepreneur Magazine Give Yourself Space to Think from Strategists Need Time to Think https://www.entrepreneur.com/article/241745 (captured February 5, 2017)

3 - How to Break a Bad Habit and Replace It With a Good One by James Clear https://jamesclear.com/how-to-break-a-bad-habit (captured July 8, 2018)

(4-) What is Happiness, Anyway? by Acacia Parks, PhD http://www.happify.com/hd/what-is-happiness-anyway (captured March 23, 2017)

(5) Write Down What You Are Grateful For (on Learning How To Stop Feeling Sorry For Yourself With Easy Steps) http://howtobehappy.guru/learning-how-to-stop-feeling-sorry-for-yourself-with-easy-steps/ (captured March 25, 2017)

(6) Is it possible for God, the creator of all things to live inside a person? by JA Pérez https://japerez.com/english/is-it-possible-for-god-the-creator-of-all-things-to-live-inside-a-person/ (captured March 25, 2017)

7- Our Deepest Prayer: Hallowed Be Your Name by

John Piper. Desiring God. http://www.desiringgod.org/messages/our-deepest-prayer-hallowed-be-your-name (captured February 19, 2017)

8- Praying for a Breakthrough by John Piper. Desiring God. http://www.desiringgod.org/articles/praying-for-a-breakthrough (captured February 19, 2017)

9- Experience the Presence: Prayer is experiencing the presence of God by The Navigators

Download PDF at: http://www.navigators.org/Tools/Prayer%20Resources/PageItems/Experience%20the%20Presence (captured February 19, 2017)

10- How to Jump Start Your Prayer Battery by Kim Butts. Harvest Prayer Ministries http://www.harvestprayer.com/resources/articles/personal/jump-start-your-prayer-battery (captured February 19, 2017)

11- Beginning a Life of Prayer by PrayerPower Radio. Download PDF at: http://www.prayerpowerministries.com/pdf/06-ARTICLE-Beginning-a-Life-of-Prayer.pdf (captured February 19, 2017)

12- Ten Minutes with the Lord: Start Where You Are by Kaye Johns. Download at: http://www.prayerpowerministries.com/pdf/09-ARTICLE-Ten-Minutes-with-the-Lord.pdf (captured February 19, 2017)

13- Prayer of Salvation: Our First Real Conversation With God by All About God. Download at: http://www.allaboutgod.com/common/printable-prayer-of-salvation.htm (captured February 19, 2017)

14- Prayer 101: How Do I Talk to God? by BGEA. https://billygraham.org/story/prayer-101-how-do-i-talk-to-god/ (captured February 19, 2017)

15- 10 Morning Prayers to Use Daily by Crosswalk Editorial Staff. http://www.crosswalk.com/faith/prayer/prayers/10-morning-prayers-to-use-daily.html (captured

February 19, 2017)

16- Seven Simple Daily Prayers by Marshall Segal. Desiring God. http://www.desiringgod.org/articles/seven-simple-daily-prayers (captured February 19, 2017)

17- How to Read the Bible by Wikihow. http://www.wikihow.com/Read-the-Bible (captured February 19, 2017)

18- How to Read the Bible by NLT. http://www.newlivingtranslation.com/02biblestudy/howtoread.asp (captured February 19, 2017)

19- The Bible in Basic English by Bible Study Tools. http://www.biblestudytools.com/bbe/ (captured February 19, 2017)

20- The Bible in One Year by Alpha International. https://www.bibleinoneyear.org/ (captured February 19, 2017)

21- Your low-limit secured card strategy: Pay the bill early, often: Time payments, use your statement date to keep credit utilization low by Barry Paperno. CreditCards.com http://www.creditcards.com/credit-card-news/low-limit-strategy-pay-early-often-1586.php (captured February 19, 2017)

22- How Many Times A Day Should You Check Your Email? By Tucker Cummings. http://www.lifehack.org/articles/productivity/how-many-times-a-day-should-you-check-your-email.html (captured February 19, 2017)

23- How many times does the average person check Email and Facebook per day? By Michael Andrew. http://www.michaelthemaven.com/index.cfm?postID=1412 (captured February 19, 2017)

24- Never Check Email in the Morning by Julie Morgenstern. ISBN: 978-0743250887 Publisher: Touchstone; Reprint edition (September 27, 2005) More about the author and the book: http://www.juliemorgenstern.com/books/neer-check-e-mail-in-the-morning (captured February 19, 2017)

25- Time management: How an MIT postdoc writes 3 books, a PhD defense, and 6+ peer-reviewed papers — and finishes by 5:30pm. Ramit Sethi · November 19th, 2009 http://www.iwillteachyoutoberich.com/blog/time-management-how-an-mit-postdoc-writes-3-books-a-phd-defense-and-6-peer-reviewed-papers-and-finishes-by-530pm/ (captured February 19, 2017)

26- This Is What The Schedules Of Successful People Look Like by Amy Johnson. http://www.lifehack.org/articles/productivity/this-what-the-schedules-successful-people-look-like.html (captured February 19, 2017)

27- Why I wake up early by Richard Branson. https://www.virgin.com/richard-branson/why-i-wake-up-early (captured February 19, 2017)

28- What Is An Enough List And How it Helped Me Enjoy Everyday by Melissa Camara Wilkins. http://storylineblog.com/2016/03/16/enough/

29- Joshua Becker. Becoming Minimalist. blog http://www.becomingminimalist.com/to-do/

30- New Study: Daily Walk Can Add 7 Years to Your Life by Dr. Mercola. http://fitness.mercola.com/sites/fitness/archive/2015/09/11/daily-walk-benefits.aspx (captured February 19, 2017)

31- A daily walk 'can add seven years to your life': Everyone should be doing at least between 20 and 25 minutes of walking a day. Independent. http://www.independent.co.uk/life-style/health-and-families/health-news/a-daily-walk-can-add-seven-years-to-your-life-10478821.html (captured February 19, 2017)

32- Walking IS as good for your health as running - but you'll need to do it for longer to get the same benefits by Jenny Hope. http://www.dailymail.co.uk/health/article-2303512/Walking-IS-good-health-running--youll-need-longer-benefits.html (captured February 19, 2017)

33- As easy as one-two-three http://idioms.thefreedictionary.com/easy+as+1-2-3 The Free Dictionary Copyright © 2003-2017 Farlex, Inc

34- Business Insider Magazine. Marketers Must Understand The Power Of Three. http://www.businessinsider.com/using-the-power-of-three-to-your-marketing-advantage-2013-5

35- Rule of three (writing). From Wikipedia, the free encyclopedia https://en.wikipedia.org/wiki/Rule_of_three_(writing)

36- Psycho-Cybernetics, A New Way to Get More Living Out of Life by Maxwell Maltz Pocket Books (August 15, 1989) ISBN 978-0671700751

37- How Long Does it Actually Take to Form a New Habit? (Backed by Science) by James Clear. http://jamesclear.com/new-habit (captured February 24, 2017)

38- How are habits formed: Modelling habit formation in the real world by Phillippa Lally. First published: 16 July 2009. http://onlinelibrary.wiley.com/doi/10.1002/ejsp.674/full (captured February 24, 2017)

Dr. JA Pérez

Author, humanitarian, world evangelist. Equally at home with entrepreneurs and international government leaders as with the poor and needy in the third world. His work reaches across generations, cultures and nations. Has written more than 50 books and assists intellectuals as well as the unschooled, in the acquisition of essential skills—and practical how-to solutions—for achieving optimal productivity without losing enjoyment and rest.

His writings and love for literature have been greatly influenced by his late grandfather, a man who was raised by monks in a monastery in the Canary Islands, Spain.

Enjoys long slow walks, and practicing the art of sitting in silence for long periods of time.

He, his wife and their three children, live in San Diego, California, from where they manage the entire scope of their organization.

Other books by JA Pérez

ENGLISH

Leadership / Collaboration Series

LATEST | SPANISH

Leadership Series

On Inspiration and Creativity for Leadership

On Finances and Economy

Faith // Discipleship

Devotionals

Fiction

On Collaboration

On Christian Life, Growth, Life Principles, and Relationships

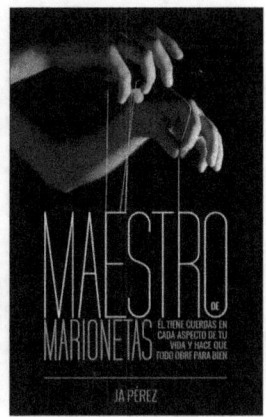

On Christian Life, Growth, Life Principles, and Relationships - Classics

Contact / follow the author

Personal blog and social medias

japerez.com/english

@japereznow

facebook.com/japereznow

KEEN SIGHT BOOKS

www.ingramcontent.com/pod-product-compliance
Lightning Source LLC
LaVergne TN
LVHW051748080426
835511LV00018B/3267